P9-DTQ-957

A Note to Parents

DK READERS is a compelling program for beginning readers, designed in conjunction with leading literacy experts, including Dr. Linda Gambrell, Director of the School of Education at Clemson University. Dr. Gambrell has served on the Board of Directors of the International Reading Association and as President of the National Reading Conference.

Beautiful illustrations and superb full-color photographs combine with engaging, easy-to-read stories to offer a fresh approach to each subject in the series. Each DK READER is guaranteed to capture a child's interest while developing his or her reading skills, general knowledge, and love of reading.

The five levels of DK READERS are aimed at different reading abilities, enabling you to choose the books that are exactly right for your child:

Pre-level 1: Learning to read
Level 1: Beginning to read
Level 2: Beginning to read alone
Level 3: Reading alone
Level 4: Proficient readers

The "normal" age at which a child begins to read can be anywhere from three to eight years old, so these levels are intended only as a general guideline.

No matter which level you select, you can be sure that you are helping your child learn to read, then read to learn!

LONDON, NEW YORK, MUNICH,
MELBOURNE, AND DELHI

Created by Leapfrog Press Ltd.
Project Editor Emma Johnson
Art Editor Andrew Burgess
For Dorling Kindersley
Senior Editor Linda Esposito
Managing Art Editor Peter Bailey
US Editor Regina Kahney
Production Josie Alabaster
Picture Researcher Liz Moore
Illustrator Tony Smith
Jacket Designer Chris Drew

Reading Consultant
Linda B. Gambrell Ph.D.

First American Edition, 1999
07 10 9 8 7 6 5 4 3
Published in the United States by DK Publishing, Inc.
375 Hudson Street, New York, New York 10014

Copyright © 1999 Dorling Kindersley Limited
All rights reserved under International and Pan-American Copyright
Conventions. No part of this publication may be reproduced, stored in a
retrieval system, or transmitted in any form or by any means, electronic,
mechanical, photocopying, recording, or otherwise, without the prior
written permission of the copyright owner.

Published in Great Britain by Dorling Kindersley Limited

Library of Congress Cataloging-in-Publication Data
Brooks, Philip, 1955–
  Invaders from outer space : real-life stories of UFOs / written by Philip Brooks. --
1st American ed.
    p. cm. -- (Dorling Kindersley readers. Level 3)
  Summary: Examines the phenomena of unidentified flying objects
and encounters with alien beings.
      ISBN-13: 978-0-7894-3999-4 (plc)
      ISBN-13: 978-0-7894-3998-7 (pb)
  1. Unidentified flying objects--Sightings and encounters--Juvenile
literature. 2. Human-alien encounters--Juvenile literature.
  [1. Unidentified flying objects. 2. Extraterrestrial beings.]
  I. Title. II. Series.
TL789.2.B76 1999
001.942--DC21   98-41848
                                                  CIP
                                                  AC

Color reproduction by Colourscan, Singapore
Printed and bound in China by L Rex Printing Co., Ltd.

The publisher would like to thank the following
for their kind permission to reproduce their photographs:
Key: t=top, b=below, l=left, r=right, c=centre
Corbis UK Ltd: 9; **Dorling Kindersley Picture Library:** 38, 42; **Mary
Evans Picture Library:** 18tr, br, 25br, 27br, 32, 34, 35cl, bl, 44cl, bl,
br, 45cl, b, 47t; **Fortean Picture Library:** 8cl, cr, 14tr, 14-15, 17tr,
19, 26, 28tr; **Galaxy Picture Library:** 27tr; **Images Colour Library:** 7tr,
22br; **National Motor Museum:** 39b; **Planet Earth:** 8br;
Popperfoto/Reuters: 47b; **David Tam:** 3, 23, 44cr; **Trip:** 47cr. Jacket:
David Tarn: front cover left.
All other images © Dorling Kindersley Limited.
For further information see: www.dkimages.com

Discover more at
www.dk.com

Contents

 **DK READERS**

READING
3
ALONE

INVADERS FROM OUTER SPACE

REAL-LIFE STORIES OF UFOs

Written by Philip Brooks

SMBSD

DK Publishing, Inc.

Where in the world?

Every year hundreds of people say they have seen Unidentified Flying Objects (UFOs) in the sky. Many believe these are spaceships from faraway galaxies, transporting aliens across space to visit our planet.

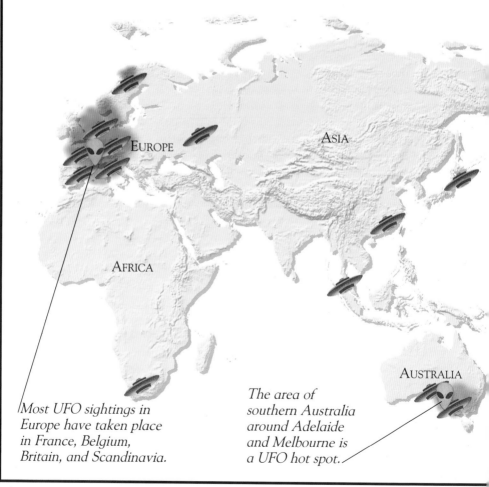

EUROPE

ASIA

AFRICA

AUSTRALIA

Most UFO sightings in Europe have taken place in France, Belgium, Britain, and Scandinavia.

The area of southern Australia around Adelaide and Melbourne is a UFO hot spot.

The map of the world below shows UFO "hot spots" – areas of the world where the most UFO sightings have been reported.

In this book you will read about some of the most famous stories ever reported of close encounters with aliens.

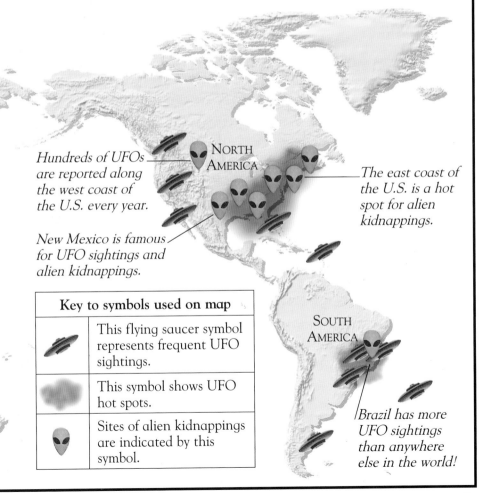

Hundreds of UFOs are reported along the west coast of the U.S. every year.

NORTH AMERICA

The east coast of the U.S. is a hot spot for alien kidnappings.

New Mexico is famous for UFO sightings and alien kidnappings.

SOUTH AMERICA

Brazil has more UFO sightings than anywhere else in the world!

Key to symbols used on map	
	This flying saucer symbol represents frequent UFO sightings.
	This symbol shows UFO hot spots.
	Sites of alien kidnappings are indicated by this symbol.

The Roswell incident

DATE: JULY 3, 1947
PLACE: ROSWELL, NEW MEXICO

William "Mac" Brazel rode his horse across the dry desert land of his ranch. He thought about the explosion he had heard last night during a storm. Now he wanted to find out what had caused it.

Something silver glinted in the sunlight, catching Mac's eye. The ground around him was littered with shiny metal pieces. He stopped to pick one up.

The fragment was extremely lightweight but unbendable. And it was covered with hieroglyphs.

Picture writing

Pictures used instead of letters to form a language are called hieroglyphs. Ancient cultures, such as the Egyptians, used them.

Mac felt uneasy. The metal looked like nothing on earth. He telephoned the airforce base at nearby Roswell.

Staff from the Roswell Base arrived at Mac's ranch. They posted guards around the area where the metal was found.

On July 8, the Airforce Base issued an amazing news statement, saying that the wreckage was from a flying saucer.

Newspaper headlines about the Roswell Incident in 1947

Weather balloon

Scientists use balloons to help them predict the weather. The balloons record air temperature and pressure high in the sky.

Later that day, the base released a second statement. It said that the first story was a mistake. The crashed object was in fact a weather balloon. But was it? Were the authorities covering something up?

Officers of the U.S Air Force identify metal found near Roswell as part of a weather balloon, not a flying saucer.

Soon there were stories of a second crash site about 100 miles (160 kms) west of Roswell. An engineer named Grady Barnett said he was working in the desert when he saw a large metal disk on the ground. Scattered around the crumpled disk were five small, gray bodies. They appeared to be dead.

As Grady stood staring, a military vehicle drove up. An officer jumped out.

He told Grady to leave at once and, more importantly, never speak about what he had seen.

As he was hustled away, Grady glanced over his shoulder. One of the creatures seemed to open an eye and look back at him.

Secrets of Hanger 84

It is thought that UFO wreckage and alien bodies from Roswell were stored in Hanger 84 on the Roswell Air Base.

Grady Barnett said later that the bodies were "like humans, but they were not humans." They were small, with spindly arms and legs. Their heads were large, with sunken eyes and no teeth.

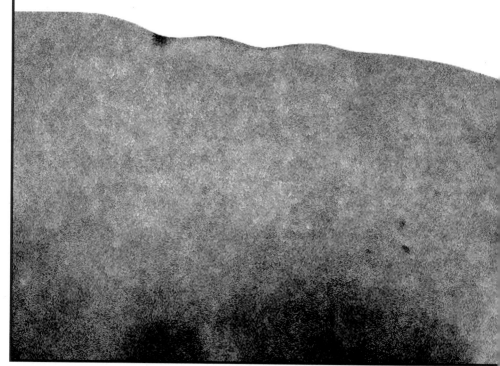

In the fifty years since the actual event, various witnesses have come forward with bizarre stories about the aliens. Some claim the alien bodies were taken to the Roswell Air Force Base.

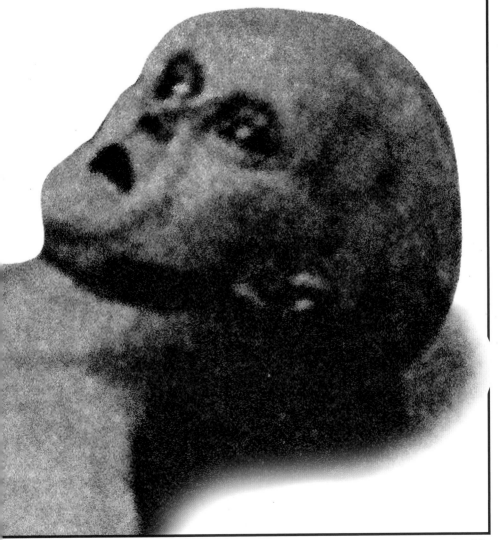

Film stills

Scenes from the film are
displayed at the UFO
Museum at Roswell.
Are they real or are
they faked?

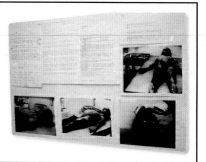

One story told how doctors at the
Roswell Army Hospital had been
ordered on duty at short notice. The
shocked doctors were told to cut open
and examine the bodies of the dead
aliens in a procedure called an autopsy.

When the bodies were cut open, a
terrible smell filled the room. Several
doctors became too sick to carry on.

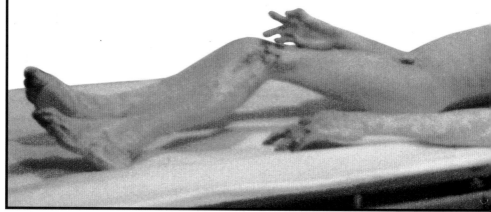

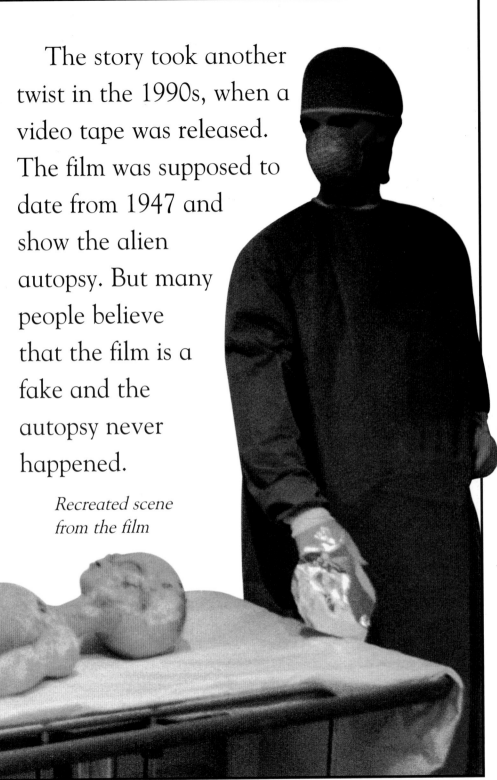

The story took another twist in the 1990s, when a video tape was released. The film was supposed to date from 1947 and show the alien autopsy. But many people believe that the film is a fake and the autopsy never happened.

Recreated scene from the film

The Roswell legend has continued to grow. New details have been added, including a rumor that the alien bodies were frozen in ice and kept at a top-secret airforce base called Area 51.

Signs warn travelers away from Area 51, north of Los Angeles. Some people claim that the U.S. army hides UFO wreckage here.

Holloman, New Mexico
Another U.S. Air Force base linked to alien activity is Holloman. This 1957 photograph seems to show a UFO above the base.

It seems certain that something did crash at Roswell in 1947. Does the air-force know more than it is telling? Were the stories fake? We may never know. ❖

WARNING
MILITARY INSTALLATION

Kidnapped by aliens

DATE: SEPTEMBER 19, 1961
PLACE: INDIAN HEAD,
NEW HAMPSHIRE

Betty and Barney Hill were driving home late at night. They had no

Betty and Barney Hill

idea that they were heading toward a terrifying encounter with the unknown.

The couple were returning from vacation along Route 3 in Indian Head, New Hampshire, when they saw a bright saucer shape in the sky. It seemed to be following their car along the road.

Lights in the sky

Throughout history there have been reports of people seeing saucer-shaped objects in the sky. This Swiss engraving is from 1566.

"Where are the binoculars? I want
to see what kind of plane that is," said
Barney as he stopped the car.

What Barney saw next both amazed
and frightened him.

Looking through his binoculars, Barney could see a pancake-shaped craft of some kind. There were flashing colored lights around its edge. And from inside the craft, a group of sinister-looking figures stared down at him.

"Hey, I can see a row of windows. There are figures inside!" reported Barney to his wife. "They're looking at us, watching us!"

Betty and Barney looked at each other in silent terror. Then Betty burst out, "I'm scared. Let's get away from it."

Their hearts pounding, the Hills got back into their car and drove off at top speed, leaving the strange craft far behind them in the night.

When they got back home, though, their troubles really began.

The Hills figured out that their journey had taken an extra two hours, but the car's odometer showed the trip had been 35 miles (56 kms) shorter than usual. Barney's shoes were badly scuffed and the paint on his car was marked with dark blotches. What had happened in the missing two hours?

Betty began having nightmares about aliens. She was certain the dreams were linked to the strange craft they'd seen. The Hills found a doctor who agreed to use hypnosis to help them remember more about what happened that night.

Hypnosis
Hypnotists, like Dr. Simon who hypnotized the Hills, put their patients into a trance to help them remember past events.

Under hypnosis, the Hills recalled
being kidnapped by short, gray creatures
with large heads and huge, dark eyes.

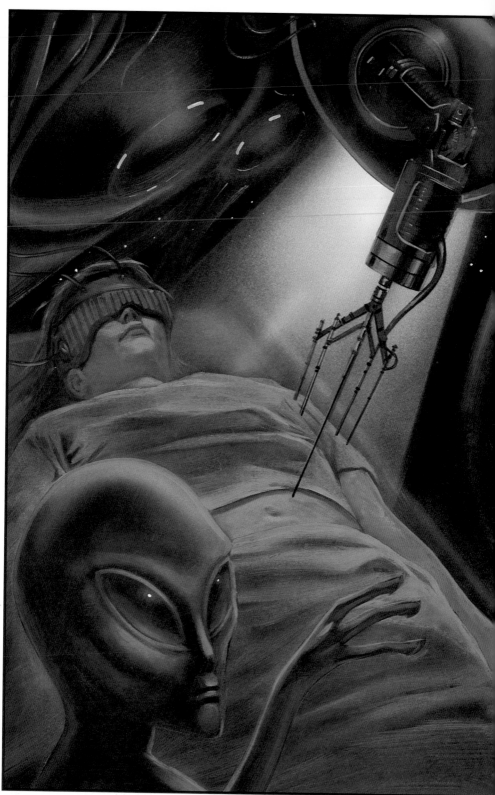

The alien beings floated Betty and Barney into their spacecraft and began to examine them.

At first the aliens were quite friendly and Betty was not afraid. They carefully took samples of the couple's hair and skin. Then they pushed a long needle into Betty's stomach near her navel. The aliens seemed particularly fascinated by Barney's false teeth.

Betty asked the creatures where they were from, and they showed her a star map displaying what they said was their home planet.

Strange marks

Many people claim they have been examined by aliens. In 1967 Steve Michalak showed marks on his chest he said were caused by vapor from a UFO.

Under hypnosis, Betty drew the star map. Many people have tried to identify the star system shown. Some researchers have suggested it shows a group of stars called Zeta Reticuli. Other people have since said they have met aliens from this group of stars.

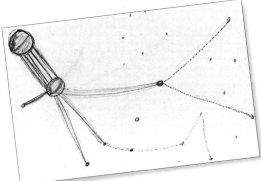

Betty Hill's star map sketch

The Hills' story has become one of America's most famous UFO cases. It was one of the earliest examples of a "spacenapping," which is now called an alien abduction.

When news of their abduction hit the headlines, many doctors and scientists questioned Betty and Barney about their mysterious encounter with aliens.

Zeta Reticuli

Did the aliens come from a group of stars named Zeta Reticuli? This star system is about 30 light-years from our sun.

Some thought the Hills' story was a fantasy or a nightmare, perhaps brought on by being hypnotized.

Others still believe that something unusual really did happen to the Hills on that lonely stretch of highway.

Betty and Barney stuck to their story and swore it was true for the rest of their lives. ❖

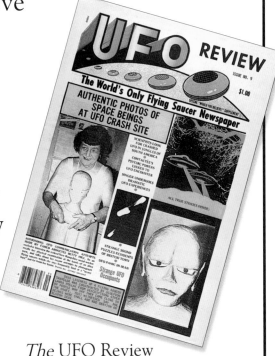

The UFO Review *features Betty Hill's story.*

Alien blast-off

DATE: APRIL 24, 1964, TIME: 5:45 PM
PLACE: SOCORRO, NEW MEXICO

Lonnie Zamora's police car raced along the highway, throwing up clouds of dust. He was

Lonnie Zamora

chasing a Chevrolet traveling way above the local speed limit.

Suddenly Lonnie caught sight of something extraordinary. A blue-orange flame blazed in the sky, then flew down behind a nearby hill.

Lonnie swerved off the road and sped cross-country to where the flame had disappeared.

As Lonnie drew nearer, he caught sight of an odd-looking object. At first he thought it was an upside-down car. He got out of his own car to look closer.

The object appeared to be an egg-shaped craft – with no doors or windows – resting on four silver legs. Near the strange craft, Lonnie saw two child-size figures dressed from head to toe in white overalls. One of the little figures caught sight of Lonnie and jumped, as if surprised to see him. Who, or what, could they be?

Lonnie got back in his car and radioed the sheriff's office for help. When he looked up again, the two figures had disappeared.

Lonnie heard loud thumps, like someone shutting doors. He approached the craft again and noticed a peculiar red symbol on the side of it. Before he could study it further, a loud blast filled the desert air.

The craft began to rise from the ground, sending up a whirlwind of dust. The engine noise changed tone but sounded nothing like a plane. Lonnie dived for cover behind a nearby ridge. He thought the craft was going to explode. But it shot off like a bullet and vanished into the sky.

Police Sergeant Sam Chavez reached Lonnie just after the craft had blasted off. Some nearby bushes were still burning. The two policemen made a thorough search of the area. They found scorch marks on the ground, together with four dents in the soil where the craft's legs had rested. They found five other marks that looked like footprints.

Sam Chavez and Lonnie Zamora inspect the site.

Marks in the ground

Inspection of the landing site showed dents in the sand where Lonnie had seen the craft. The marks were about 2-3 inches (8-12 cm) deep.

Soon after this, another witness reported seeing an egg-shaped craft. On April 26, Orlando Gallego saw one land at La Madera, New Mexico. Police officers found evidence of burning where Gallego said the craft had landed. They also found four round prints in the soil, just as they had at Socorro.

On April 28, an official team of investigators led by Dr. Allen Hynek came to Socorro to learn about what Lonnie had seen. Dr. Hynek was a top scientist working for the U.S. Air Force on Project Blue Book (PBB).

Project Blue Book was the U.S. Air Force's own file on UFOs. Between 1952 and 1969 the Blue Book investigators examined more than 13,000 reports and photographs of UFOs.

In Socorro, Hynek checked that no aerospace company was privately developing an egg-shaped airplane.

UFO investigators from Project Blue Book pose for a photograph. The man seated is Major Quintanilla of the U.S. Air Force, who was one of the heads of the project.

His team also checked that the craft wasn't a Lunar Exploration Module, designed to travel on the moon.

Hynek described Lonnie as honest and reliable and believed he was telling the truth. Project Blue Book labeled what he had seen as "unidentified." To this day, it has not been explained. ❖

Project Blue Book found this photograph to be a fake. Modern investigators are less sure.

Project Blue Book proved this 1960s photograph, taken in New Mexico, shows a model UFO.

This photograph was declared a fake by Project Blue Book.

The Men in Black

DATE: 1950S UNTIL TODAY
PLACE: WORLDWIDE

Robert Richardson was driving through Ohio late one summer evening in 1967. As he rounded a bend, he saw a bright, glowing object blocking the road in front of him. He could not brake in time.

Robert hit the object, which promptly vanished. He was shaken and dazed. Had he collided with an alien spacecraft?

Searching the crash site later, Robert found a piece of dull silver metal from the object. He sent the metal to UFO researchers and thought that would be the end of the incident.

He was wrong.

A few days later, at 11 o'clock in the evening, two men appeared at Robert's home. They were wearing dark suits with white shirts and black ties. Everything about the men seemed menacing. They did not tell Robert who they were.

The men tried to persuade Robert that the crash had never happened. When he stuck to his story, they became angry and said his wife would suffer if he didn't give them the metal.

As the men drove away in a black Cadillac, Robert made note of their license number. He was frightened enough to get in touch with the UFO researchers and ask them to return the metal to him. But the Men in Black never came back. And when he checked the car's license plate, he found that it had never been issued.

Black Cadillac

Men in Black are often said to arrive in big black cars in perfect condition. In the U.S. these are usually Cadillacs.

Another strange Men in Black incident happened in September 1976. Dr. Herbert Hopkins, who was investigating a UFO abduction in Maine, received a visit from a man dressed in a black suit and tie.

Human or alien?

Dr. Hopkins' visitor seemed not quite human. Some people believe that Men in Black are aliens dressed to look like government agents.

The man's skin was unnaturally white and his lips were bright red. He was completely bald.

He talked for a little while about UFOs. Then he pulled a coin from his pocket and made it fade out of focus and vanish in front of the doctor's eyes.

"Neither you nor anyone else on this planet will see that coin again," he said.

The strange man warned Dr. Hopkins that he should stop working with UFO witnesses. Then he left.

Dr. Hopkins was so frightened that he gave up his UFO work forever.

Men in Black have been seen all over the world, but there are no known cases in which they have carried out their threats.

Many think they are a product of people's imaginations. But reports of them worldwide are strangely similar. Can so many independent witnesses have made up the same things?

Some people think the Men in Black are government officials trying to find out more about UFO witnesses. They sometimes show government identity cards. But no government department will admit that they exist.

The Men in Black are as mysterious as they are menacing.

If you see a UFO, be warned – you may get a visit from a Man in Black! ❖

Aliens: the fact file

The alien encounters in this book are just a few of thousands reported in the last fifty years. Here are some of the aliens and UFOs most frequently described by people – and some of the most bizarre. ❖

Grays

Betty and Barney Hill (page 18) were captured by Grays – small, human-shaped creatures with pale gray skin. Grays are the most commonly seen aliens.

Gobblens

These are green, goblin-like aliens with short legs and long arms. Their heads are abnormally large with pointed ears and bulging eyes.

One-legged aliens

In 1977, a Brazilian bus driver reported seeing a tall alien with a pointed head and one leg. It had arms like elephants' trunks.

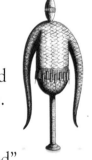

Nordics

Some people claim they were "spacenapped" by tall aliens with yellow hair. These aliens look human, but can change their body shape or become beams of light.

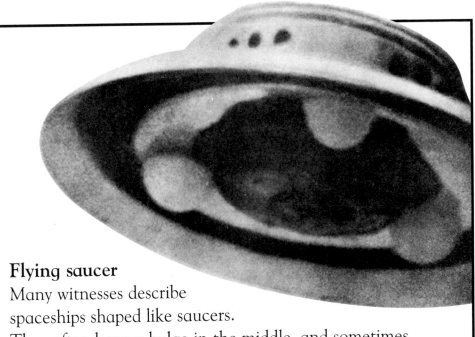

Flying saucer

Many witnesses describe
spaceships shaped like saucers.
They often have a bulge in the middle, and sometimes
rows of windows. Grady Barnett (page 10) and the Hills
(page 18) described seeing this kind of craft.

Glowing spheres

UFO witnesses have often reported
ball-shaped spaceships. Sometimes these
ships are said to glow orange or yellow.

Egg-shaped craft

This kind of craft was best described by Lonnie
Zamora in his encounter (page 28). Other
witnesses describe white or blue egg-shaped
craft that are covered with strange markings.

Cigar-shaped ship

Long, silver-colored UFOs are often reported.
These may be motherships, because smaller craft often
appear to be accompanying them.

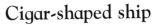

True or false?

Investigators explain away UFOs by saying they are unusual weather conditions or secret military aircraft. But for one in ten sightings, no one can find an earthly explanation. ❖

Lenticular clouds

Lenticular (len-TICK-you-ler), or lens-shaped, clouds are often mistaken for flying saucers. Rarely seen, they stay still for long periods. These are above Santos, in Brazil.